Life Goes On

Yacob Laine

BookLeaf Publishing

India | USA | UK

Presentation by *BookLeaf Publishing*

Web: www.bookleafpub.com

E-mail: info@bookleafpub.com

ISBN: 9789357445719

First edition 2022

DEDICATION

To Mama, my siblings and those along the way who lent a helping hand in life when needed. Last but not least, to get this far is by God's grace.

PREFACE

Most of these poems were written for a 21-day poem challenge that led to the publication of this book. Some ("Blue", "Divinity", "The Pairs of Words" and "The Value of a Dream") were written for a class assignment, hence the difference in style and format. With such poems, re-formatting them would significantly alter their essence. With that in mind, enjoy the book!

Poem #1

Moving at the speed of light
like you're in the middle of space
but when it's time to write
that's when the race
ends, the plethora of thoughts
shutting off like a faucet.
Brains are funny.
You have something on your mind,
but it runs away from you
like when you forget to pick up
something from the store
 when it was your
main reason for going there
and you don't realize until you're
somewhere close to home.
That's what it's like writing this,
the grand wonder that is
the world slipping my mind
like sand through fingers.
It's better to keep moving and
keep creating than to allow perfectionism
to linger
and linger
and linger.

Times Square

The hustle and bustle of the city
personified, the scenes just like on TV.
The beautiful and gritty
Home of the New Year's Eve Ball Drop
and so much more. If you just stop
and stare, you'll see why
scores of people
near and far come there.
A pedestrian oasis in the heart of Midtown,
surrounded by cars, trucks, people
all with somewhere to be,
something to do, a living to make,
and an American dream to chase.
The pit of the melting pot,
The 5 Boroughs, Jersey, out-of-towners,
foreigners and immigrants,
all represented, sharing the same space.
From the street performers to the
costumed folk to the immigrant street
vendors, photographers and everyone in
between,
Lo and behold: Times Square.

Island

An island, a body of land
completely surrounded by water.
I reckon all of us are walking islands,
surrounded by the waters of individuality and
uniqueness,
a life path that leaves us alone
at the end of the day.
Some of us are bona fide islands,
entities anonymous, removed from others,
isolated
from others. Some of us are like archipelagos,
part of a larger group of connected islands.
Some of us were brought up to embrace our
island status; others were brought up to connect
and conform to the archipelago.
Here's the thing, though: even in the busiest
areas, we are all islands just going about tending
to the affairs of our individual lives.
Consider communication, culture, camaraderie,
and family to
be like the vessels that travel from one island to
the next. I guess that's why they say
"Build bridges" or "Don't burn bridges".
See, now it all makes sense.

The Invisible Wall

Mothers and fathers, sons and daughters
not on the same page,
different philosophies on life.
Any old day becomes an opportunity to wage
Civil War, driven by the division caused by
The Invisible Wall.
Philosophies about the ideal husband or wife,
how to make a buck,
what language to use, what to wear, advice
fueled by lost hopes and dreams, stuck
in a feedback loop of an interrupted life.
The recipient of said advice preoccupied with
the particulars
of figuring out their place in the new country,
hundreds or thousands of miles from
the homeland of the previous generation, who
were
blessed with clarity of identity from childhood,
but separated from what they've known.
Neither fully of the old country nor of the new
country,
both generations constrained by The Invisible
Wall
clash due to the different ways

each one is floating in uncertainty.
The particulars of each society,
their social fabrics
coming in constant conflict.
The understanding, lost in translation,
the fears of an extinct culture
somewhere down the family line.
The young ones expected to follow norms
of countries they might have never lived in.
Curse the situation, that put
within families
The Invisible Wall.

The Sphere

The fabrics of the world,
stitched together in this round object,
a universal pearl
this sphere.
Played with the most hi-tech version
or from bags, socks, whatever you can find,
tied together with a rubber band
that makes this wonderful sphere appear.
Oh what a joy! Good times,
all thanks to this spherical object.
Many an hour were spent
messing about with it,
a way to travel the world
without hopping on a plane.
The original social medium for sure.
Whoever brought it, ran the show
on playgrounds the world over,
the mass of bodies running, chasing
this spherical object to get to it first.
From kids to adults, schoolyards to the World
Cup
and everything in between,
this spherical object is a least common
denominator, an LCD.

Whether you call it soccer, calcio, football or fútbol,
A "GOOOOOOOOOOOOL!" is still a goal.

Tomorrow, Today

Tomorrow has come today!
The different bright yellow, red and orange hues
of a new day. The symbol of progress,
hopes and dreams for a better time,
Vitamin D, happiness, liveliness all hitting
your skin. Oh, how you are cause for
celebrations, festivals, joy galore.
The first days of spring, the first days of
summer,
the end of a long school year or
just the end of a long winter,
seeing the masses out and about,
the young ones running,
their audible shouts.
The days are longer, the weather warmer.
The streetlights come later, more time to savor
the outdoors, before you have to come home.
People up and go to places far, far away
just to feel more of your warm embrace.
I tell you, Christmas with you at the function
is a weird thought, but maybe not for others.
This warm blanket, wrapping around you,
one that you can count on coming day in, day
out.

Whether you see her or not,
she'll be there.

Light in the Night Sky

Whenever I would travel,
I thought you used to travel with me.
So imagine how baffled
I was when I found out otherwise.
We're moving? Not you?
It was so hard to imagine
us moving around a rotating world
when we stand so still,
firmly attached to the ground,
with no indication of a moving world
other than the passing of the world
outside of the car.
Lighting up the night sky,
you look so close, yet you're so far.
To get to where you are,
would require more planning than a day trip.
So bright, different shapes
for different nights
make for a picturesque scene.
Whether sitting on top of a sky
filled with the bright lights

of a city or the only light
in the pitch black of the country,
your intrigue is quite powerful.

Smells

Warmth, heat, light, cooking.
The smell of the charcoal
and the burning wood
traveling down the block,
the smoke in the air
wafting into your nostrils.
The scenes of cooking turning
into a public spectacle,
part of the community landscape
as people go about their daily lives.
A communal experience, indeed.
From the neighborhood ladies
to the street vendors
trying to get you to
buy some corn,
it's everywhere.
The memories are ever so present,
back to the basics we go.
Science, art, intuition
all merging to make a
creation out of simple
ingredients, bringing the dish
to life. Simple, yet complex.

Blue

Blue is such a peaceful color, with
light blue the hue of the sky.
Blue is such a powerful color
representing an entire emotion.

Blue is for boys,
a color in which babies are
announced to the world.
Blue is lifelike,
a symbol for water.

Blue is so expansive.
The numerous uses for this color,
the different stories it tells
and the different meanings-
Here's to blue.

Scribbles

Parading around a piece of paper,
child's play apparent in
loose and chaotic marks,
a series of lifeless motions bring
an artwork to life.
Controlled disorganization,
producing a coherent image,
makes for a cathartic release.
Freedom of movement for the
hand, as opposed to the taxing
concentration of realism or
the monotony of pointillism.
Maybe it's just me,
but the unpredictability
of the strokes in a
non-abstract artwork
makes for an interesting time.
Fading away from the subject,
the lines protruding from each side,
making the subject look like a
heartbeat. That would be nice.
Yeah, it would.

Grow Up

From birth, with all of your fresh vitality
crying loudly, you announce your arrival.
Or not, delaying your announcement until
the midwife or the doctor taps the baby to life.
A baby who grows up to be a toddler,
starting to crawl, then walk, then talk,
then play with all of the other
little beings born around the same time
as them, friends, sisters, brothers
all running in childlike simplicity,
until it's time for school,
or work for those who need to support their
families.
Then, they mature, and become
young adults. Goodness, you wake
up one day and hit your 20s,
thrust into the machine of life,
gearing up to handle business, which
soon turns into running the show and
teaching the next generation the
ropes. I'm only 23. How am I
supposed to do all of this?

Laughter

Lol! Kkkkkk ¡Jajajaja!
Sounds of laughter
erupting, bursting across the
screen leaving you with
the image of unrestrained
amusement, where the
stresses of life are
checked at the door
(if only temporarily).
Where rhyme and reason
leave temporarily,
purely ecstatic energy
emanating. They say
laughter is the best medicine.
Now, I don't know about that,
but it can help deal
with this life of sin.
It can lift you up when
you're down, turn that frown
upside down and pass the
time with good company
in the house or
out on the town.
What a wonder it is, indeed.

Celebration

The release of energy,
the equilibrium in your
body being reset
with every movement,
whether alone or in the
middle of a crowd.
The joy palpable, the music loud,
the feet moving, the worries
of the world cast aside like
shoes at the door of a house.
Lifting your spirits
up to Cloud 9,
step by step,
each step on the ground
propels you to peak enjoyment.
A practice, different across time
and place, yet the glee is
universal. From the aba guayla to
the DJs, guayla to salsa to soul
and everything in between.
You don't need
a translator to understand the
joy and celebration surrounding
such scenes.

Perfection

Perfection is an ideal
out of the reach
of the average mere mortal
roaming this Earth.
It is a but a portal
of inhibition, inertia,
the sort of inaction that can lead
to a life not fully lived.
It is like a low-hanging
 fruit, easy enough to see,
to visualize but seemingly
out of reach for our human fallibility.
Too much this, not enough that,
 perfection
is a rarity that occurs just
enough to keep us chasing it
like a bigger payday for a gambler
or a thrill for adrenaline junkies.
Some may say perfection is a mindset,
one of the pursuit of excellence,
material and spiritual,
A feeling of wholeness or completion
to remedy feelings of emptiness
within us.

Perfect

Perfect: flawless, absolute,
complete. Well, the truth
 is I don't know
 who will ever be so.
A lofty ideal,
a great distance to go
to get to that destination.
It's worth a try.
The pursuit of perfection
always leaves room for
improvement. Isn't that what
confession is for?
Isn't that why people pray,
to make themselves whole,
pure, PERFECT,
despite their imperfections?
The quest to be perfect,
will be worth it,
when you seek progress and improvement.
Isn't that
what practice is for, to
get us as close to perfect as
possible? It's all about progress,
not perfection.

Two Cents

"Here's my two cents," someone
will say. Or maybe it'll be
something to that effect.
Throwing in their contributions
to a conversation, on occasion
unwanted. Maybe it's to project
wisdom, maybe to hear their
own voice, maybe because they're
asked. Regardless, they throw their
two cents in amongst the loud
cacophony of sounds emanating.
Large group, small group,
it doesn't matter because
when there's a will, there's a way
and the most basic of social interactions
turns into a battle of wills.
It's about who can get their two cents in first.
Or it can be in the form of
friendly advice, a chance to live through
you. Or it could be a one-on-one,
a chance to mold the young minds
of the next generation. Regardless,
do what you will with it,
that's just my two cents.

Mirror, Mirror

Mirror mirror on the wall,
who's the harshest truth-teller
of them all?
Who is the most loyal
 friend of them all?
Who else can show you
the truth, the whole truth and
nothing but the truth
when looking at you?
Whether it's something stuck
in between your teeth
or a messed up haircut,
who else can
be the bearer of bad news like you?
Who else can lift me up
when I look nice, to admire
the splendor of a well-put
together appearance?
Mirror mirror on the wall,
the one you try
clothes on in front of
at the mall.
Mirror, mirror on the wall...

Pretentious

Why are poems pretentious,
people pretentious,
using flowery language
or complex words
to convey ideas?
Why do people think
they're a bunch of geniuses
because they use
more advanced words?
I thought it was
supposed to be your
ability to handle business,
fix problems, navigate
life, navigate expeditions.
Big words and sophisticated
language aren't necessarily
pretentious, but if they're used
to substitute knowledge for
fluff, then that's disingenuous.
Necessity is the mother
of invention, so fancy prose
doesn't necessarily say much.
Lack of education does not
mean lack of smarts.
Don't be so pretentious.

The Pairs of Words

Words hurt really bad.
Words can make people terribly sad.

Words can be ironclad and rigid.
They can be soft like a delicate touch.

If said in anger, words can hurt someone.
They can also make a friend out of a stranger.

They can be completely sappy.
Most importantly, they can make someone
happy.

Words can be just words.
Last but not least, they can grow wings and take
flight like a bird.

Divinity

The divinity of the white rays
sneaking through the tight
windows of the church
were, in retrospect,

Staples of childhood
and a lovely sight indeed.
The skies always seemed
to be blue and bright

On those Sundays as a kid
I used to loathe waking up early
to praise a God I couldn't see.
It was a lovely sight indeed.

The contrast would be ever so present
when compared to the dark brown
wood (or brick or whatever) infrastructure of
churches
everywhere with the surreal tinge

of the hue of the yellow haloed crown of Christ,
and the juxtaposition of such warm
and cool colors inside.
Alas, it was quite a lovely sight indeed.

The Value of a Dream

If you believe it with all your heart
it will come true, because my friend,
a dream is only the start for the bold.

They say get all the riches that can be sold
because after all, I wanna know when
a dream is worth more than gold.

To see it unfold like a work of art
and turn into reality makes it a godsend.
A dream is only the start for the bold.

"Money makes the world go round", I was told.
But it can't buy happiness, and
a dream is worth more than gold.

It will take you far,
but not to the end.
A dream is only the start for the bold.

You must be brave and roll

the dice,
because not much matters when you're old
except that dream worth more than gold.

www.ingramcontent.com/pod-product-compliance
Lightning Source LLC
LaVergne TN
LVHW021341200726
843509LV00014B/2620